The Plant-Based Di Beginners

Quick and easy recipes

Author

Mary M. Sanders

Roasted Red Pepper Penne with a Creamy Sauce Stuffed Acorn Squash Buddha Bowls Sun-Dried Tomato Risotto Rigatoni Zucchini "Meatballs"

Classic Stuffed Peppers Sweet Potato Salad Harvest Chicken Casserole White Chicken Chili Balsamic Glazed Chicken Turkey Bolognese Teriyaki Tempeh Lettuce Wraps How To Cook Acorn Squash

Cajun-style Vegan Red Beans & Rice Black Bean Power Bowl with Avocado Pesto

Peanutty Quinoa Bowls for Two + The Ultimate Vegan Protein Burrito How to Make Roasted Cauliflower Veggie Kebabs With Baked Tofu and Balsamic Glaze

Herb-Smothered Cannellini Beans Sag Aloo Sweet Potato and Chickpea Curry Sweet Potato Falafel Vegan Pulled Jackfruit Burger Vegan Lentil Lasagne Best-Ever Lentil Salad

Introduction

The finest cuisine is comfort food. It's hearty, full, and tasty, thanks to the butter, cream, and cheese it normally contains. It doesn't have to be that way, however. In reality, vegan comfort food can be delicious!

So, whether you're a vegetarian, vegan, or simply trying to save money by cutting down on meat and dairy, these dishes are perfect.

Diet Vegan

Veganism is a way of life that tries to avoid all types of animal exploitation and suffering, whether for food, clothing, or any other reason.

As a result, all animal products, including meat, eggs, and dairy, are excluded from the vegan diet. For many reasons, people opt to eat a vegan diet.

These issues normally span from ethics to the environment, but they may also arise from a desire to enhance one's health.

Vegan Diets in a Variety of Forms

Vegan diets come in many distinct flavors. The following are the most prevalent.

- Vegan diet centered on entire plant foods such as fruits, vegetables, whole grains, legumes, nuts, and seeds.

• Vegan raw-food diet: A vegan diet consisting of raw fruits, vegetables, nuts, seeds, or plant foods cooked at temperatures below 118°F (48°C).

• The 80/10/10 diet is a raw-food vegan diet that focuses on raw fruits and soft greens rather than fat-rich vegetables like nuts and avocados. Low-fat, raw-food vegan or fruitarian diets are other terms for the same thing.

• The starch solution: A low-fat, high-carb vegan diet similar to the 80/10/10 but focusing on cooked starches such as potatoes, rice, and maize rather than fruit.

• Raw till 4 p.m.: A low-fat vegan diet based on the 80/10/10 and starch solution Raw foods are eaten until 4 p.m., with a prepared plant-based meal available for evening.

• The thrive diet is a vegan raw-food diet. Plant-based, entire foods are eaten raw or prepared at moderate temperatures by followers.

• Junk-food Vegan diet: a vegan diet that is devoid of whole plant meals and primarily reliant on fake meats and cheeses, fries, vegan desserts, and other highly processed vegan foods.

Despite the fact that there are numerous forms of vegan diets, most scientific study does not distinguish between them.

Vegan diets may aid weight loss.

Vegans have a lower BMI and are leaner than non-vegans.

This might explain why more individuals are turning to vegan diets to reduce weight.

Other than nutrition, other variables may account for some of the weight-loss advantages vegans enjoy. Healthy lifestyle choices, such as physical exercise, as well as other health-related habits, may be among them.

Vegan diets, on the other hand, are more successful for weight reduction than the diets they are compared to in multiple randomized controlled trials that adjust for these external influences.

Even when whole-food-based diets are utilized as controls, the weight reduction advantage remains.

The American Dietetics Association (ADA), the American Heart Association (AHA), and the National Cholesterol Education Program (NCEP) all suggest certain diets (NCEP).

Furthermore, studies show that vegans lose more weight than those on calorie-restricted diets, even when they are permitted to eat until they are satisfied.

A greater dietary fiber intake, which may help you feel fuller, may contribute to the natural propensity to consume less calories on a vegan diet.

Type 2 Diabetes, Vegetarian Diets, and Blood Sugar

A vegan diet may aid in the control of blood sugar and the prevention of type 2 diabetes.

Vegans have lower blood sugar levels, greater insulin sensitivity, and a 78% reduced risk of type 2 diabetes than non-vegans, according to many studies.

Furthermore, vegan diets are said to reduce blood sugar levels in diabetics by up to 2.4 times more than the ADA, AHA, and NCEP-recommended diets.

The increased fiber consumption, which may help to reduce the blood sugar response, might explain some of the gain. The capacity of a vegan diet to reduce blood sugar levels may be enhanced by its weight-loss benefits.

The Heart and Vegan Diets

Veganism may be beneficial to your heart.

Vegans may have a 75% reduced risk of high blood pressure and a 42% lower chance of dying from heart disease, according to observational research.

The gold standard in research is randomized controlled trials, which add to the evidence.

Vegan diets, according to many studies, are much more successful than other diets for lowering blood sugar, LDL, and total cholesterol.

These benefits might be particularly advantageous since lowering blood pressure, cholesterol, and blood sugar levels can decrease the risk of heart disease by up to 46%.

Vegan Diets' Other Health Advantages

Vegan diets have been linked to a slew of other health advantages, including:

• Cancer risk: Vegans have a 15% reduced chance of getting cancer or dying from it.

• Arthritic: Vegan diets seem to be especially beneficial in lowering arthritis symptoms including pain, joint swelling, and morning stiffness.

• Kidney function: Diabetics who consume more plant protein instead of meat may have a lower risk of kidney disease.

• Alzheimer's disease: Observational research suggest that certain features of a vegan diet may help lessen the risk of Alzheimer's disease. Keep in mind, however, that the majority of the research that support these advantages are observational. This makes it impossible to say if the advantages were produced directly by the vegan diet. Before significant results may be drawn, randomized controlled trials are required.

Vegans abstain from consuming any animal products or meals containing animal-derived substances. These are a few examples:

• Beef, lamb, hog, veal, horse, organ meat, wild meat, chicken, turkey, goose, duck, quail, and other fowl

• Fish and seafood: anchovies, shrimp, squid, scallops, calamari, mussels, crab, lobster, and so on.

• Dairy products include milk, yogurt, cheese, butter, cream, ice cream, and so on.

• Eggs from chickens, quails, ostriches, fish, and other animals

• Bee products, such as honey, pollen, and royal jelly

• Whey, casein, lactose, egg white albumen, gelatin, cochineal or carmine, isinglass, shellac, L-cysteine, animal-derived vitamin D3, and fish-derived omega-3 fatty acids are all animal-based components.

Vegans that are health-conscious replace animal products with plant-based alternatives such as:

• Tofu, tempeh, and seitan: These adaptable protein-rich alternatives to meat, fish, chicken, and eggs may be used in a wide variety of dishes.

• Legumes: Foods like beans, lentils, and peas are high in nutrients and plant components. Nutrient absorption may be improved by sprouting, fermenting, and properly cooking.

• Unblanched and unroasted nuts and nut butters, which are high in iron, fiber, magnesium, zinc, selenium, and vitamin E.

• Seeds, particularly hemp, chia, and flaxseeds, which are high in protein and omega-3 fatty acids.

• Calcium-fortified plant milks and yogurts: These help vegans meet their daily calcium requirements. When feasible, choose kinds that are additionally fortified with vitamins B12 and D.

• Algae: Spirulina and chlorella are superb complete protein sources. Other types are high in iodine.

• Nutritional yeast: This is a simple method to add protein to vegan foods while also adding a cheesy taste. When feasible, choose kinds that have been fortified with vitamin B12.

• Whole grains, cereals, and pseudocereals: These foods are high in complex carbohydrates, fiber, iron, B vitamins, and minerals. High-protein foods include spelt, teff, amaranth, and quinoa.

• Sprouted and fermented plant foods: Probiotics and vitamin K2 may be found in Ezekiel bread, tempeh, miso, natto, sauerkraut, pickles, kimchi, and kombucha. Mineral absorption may be improved by sprouting and fermenting foods.

• Fruits and vegetables: These are both excellent sources of vitamins and minerals. Iron and calcium are especially abundant in leafy greens including bok choy, spinach, kale, watercress, and mustard greens.

How to Reduce the Risks

Everyone, not only vegans, benefits from a well-planned diet that avoids processed foods in favor of nutrient-dense alternatives.

Those who follow a vegan diet that isn't well-planned, on the other hand, are more vulnerable to nutritional inadequacies.

Vegans are more likely to have low amounts of vitamin B12, vitamin D, long-chain omega-3s, iodine, iron, calcium, and zinc in their blood, according to research.

Not obtaining enough of these nutrients is concerning for everyone, but it is more dangerous for people who have higher needs, such as youngsters or pregnant or lactating women.

Your capacity to get the nutrients you need from a vegan diet may be influenced by your genetic makeup and the composition of your gut flora.

Limiting the quantity of processed vegan meals you eat and replacing them with nutrient-dense plant foods is one method to reduce your risk of deficiency.

Foods fortified with calcium, vitamin D, and vitamin B12, in particular, should be consumed on a regular basis.

Vegans can also attempt fermenting, sprouting, and boiling meals if they wish to improve their iron and zinc absorption.

Additionally, cooking with iron cast pots and pans, avoiding tea or coffee with meals, and mixing iron-rich foods with a source of vitamin C may help to increase iron absorption.

In addition, include seaweed or iodized salt in a vegan's diet may help them meet their iodine requirements.

Finally, meals rich in alpha-linolenic acid (ALA) may aid in the production of longer-chain omega-3s like eicosapentaenoic acid (EPA) and docosahexaenoic acid (DHA) (DHA).

Chia, hemp, flaxseeds, walnuts, and soybeans are some of the foods that are rich in ALA. However, whether this conversion is efficient enough to suit everyday demands is a point of contention.

As a result, taking an algal oil supplement with 200–300 mg of EPA and DHA daily may be a safer strategy to avoid low levels.

Consider the Supplements

Some vegans may struggle to consume enough of the nutrient-dense or fortified foods listed above to fulfill their daily nutritional needs.

The following supplements may be very helpful in this situation:

• Vitamin B12 (cyanocobalamin): This type of vitamin B12 has been examined the most and seems to be effective for the majority of individuals.

• Vitamin D: Choose from Nordic Naturals or Viridian's D2 or vegan D3 supplements.

• Algal oil provides the EPA and DHA.

• Iron: Only if a verified shortage is present should it be supplied. Too much iron in supplements may create health problems and prevent other minerals from being absorbed.

• Iodine: Take a supplement or eat half a teaspoon of iodized salt per day.

• Calcium: Calcium is best absorbed in 500 mg or smaller dosages at a time. When calcium is taken with iron or zinc supplements, the absorption of these nutrients may be reduced.

• Zinc (zinc gluconate or zinc citrate) is a mineral that may be taken in two forms: gluconate and citrate. Calcium supplements must not be taken at the same time.

For One Week, a Vegan Sample Menu

Here's a basic menu plan for a week of vegan meals to get you started: Monday

• Breakfast: Tofu, lettuce, tomato, turmeric, and a plant-milk chai latte on a vegan breakfast sandwich

• Lunch: Peanut-dressed spiralized zucchini and quinoa salad

• Red lentil and spinach dal with wild rice for dinner. Tuesday

• Overnight oats with fruit, fortified plant milk, chia seeds, and almonds for breakfast

• Sandwich made with seitan and sauerkraut for lunch

• Pasta with a lentil bolognese sauce and a side salad for dinner. Wednesday

- Breakfast: A banana-flaxseed-walnut muffin with a mango and spinach smoothie prepared with fortified plant milk.

- For lunch, a baked tofu sandwich with tomato salad on the side.

- Dinner: Amaranth-based vegan chili Thursday: Whole-grain bread with hazelnut butter, banana, and fortified plant yogurt for breakfast.

- Lunch: Vegetable-and-tofu noodle soup

- Dinner: lettuce, corn, beans, cashews, and guacamole in a sweet potato jacket. Friday • Breakfast: Vegan chickpea and onion omelet with fortified plant milk and a cappuccino.

- Mango-pineapple salsa vegan tacos for lunch

Tempeh stir-fry with broccoli and bok choy for dinner Saturday

- Breakfast: A spinach and tofu sandwich with fortified plant milk.

- Lunch: Soup with spiced red lentils, tomato, and kale, served with whole-grain bread and hummus.

- Sushi rolls with vegetables, miso soup, edamame, and wakame salad for dinner • Breakfast on Sunday: chickpea pancakes with guacamole and salsa, as well as a glass of fortified orange juice.

- Vegan tofu quiche with sautéed mustard greens for lunch.

- Spring rolls (vegan) for dinner

Variate your protein and vegetable sources throughout the day, since each supplies various vitamins and minerals that are beneficial to your health.

In Restaurants, How to Eat Vegan

As a vegan, dining out may be difficult.

If you're going to a non-vegan restaurant, look up the menu online ahead of time to see what vegan choices are available.

When you phone ahead, the chef may sometimes prepare something special for you. This gives you the assurance that you'll be able to order something more exciting than a side salad when you arrive at the restaurant.

If you're selecting a restaurant on the fly, be sure to inquire about vegan alternatives as soon as you walk in, preferably before you're seated.

When in doubt, go to a restaurant that serves ethnic cuisine. They offer a lot of vegan-friendly foods or dishes that can easily be made vegan. Restaurants that provide Mexican, Thai, Middle Eastern, Ethiopian, and Indian cuisines are popular choices.

Once you've arrived at the restaurant, look for vegetarian alternatives on the menu and inquire whether the meal can be made vegan-friendly by removing the dairy or eggs.

To build a dinner, order a variety of vegan appetizers or side dishes.

Vegan Snacks that are both tasty and good for you

Snacks are a terrific strategy to keep yourself energetic and avoid hunger in between meals. Here are a few vegan choices that are easy to carry:

• A spoonful of nut butter with fresh fruit

• Hummus with veggies

• Roasted chickpeas • Nut and fruit bars • Nutritional yeast sprinkled over popcorn

• Mixture for the trail

• Pudding made with chia

- Cereal with plant milk • Whole-wheat pita with salsa and guacamole

- Edamame • Cashew nut spread • Whole-grain crackers

- Latte or cappuccino made with plant milk

- Snacks made with dried kelp

When making a vegan snack, choose items that are high in fiber and protein, since they will help you stay fuller for longer.

INGREDIENTS FOR THE BEST-EVEN Vegan Meatloaf

- 1/2 yellow onion, coarsely chopped • 1 tbsp. extra-virgin olive oil

- finely chopped celery (2 stalks)

- peeled and coarsely chopped 1 medium carrot

1 cup baby bella mushrooms, coarsely chopped

- drained and rinsed chickpeas from 2 (15-oz) cans

- 1 cup breadcrumbs (panko)

- 1/4 cup parsley, plus more for garnish

- 2 tablespoons soy sauce (low sodium)

- Vegan Worcestershire sauce (1 tbsp.)

- ketchup, 1/4 c.

- a quarter-cup of barbecue sauce

- Kosher salt and 1/2 teaspoon smoked paprika

- Black pepper, freshly ground Preheat the oven to 375°F and line a 5" × 8" loaf pan with parchment paper. Heat the oil in a big skillet over medium heat. Cook, stirring occasionally, for 6 to 8 minutes, or until the onion, celery, carrot, and mushrooms are tender and most of the liquid has evaporated.

- Mash the chickpeas with a potato masher until a rough puree forms in a large bowl or food processor. (A few of big chickpea chunks are OK.) If you're using a food processor, transfer the mixture to a big mixing basin.

- In the same bowl as the chickpeas, combine the cooked veggies, bread crumbs, parsley, soy sauce, and Worcestershire sauce. Combine ketchup and barbecue sauce in a medium mixing basin. 12 cup

Add this to the chickpeas in the mixing basin. Stir in the paprika, salt, and pepper until all of the ingredients are well combined.

• Gently put the chickpea mixture into the loaf pan. Bake for 30 minutes after smoothing the top with half of the leftover ketchup mixture. Remove from oven and brush with leftover ketchup mixture before baking for another 30 minutes.

• Allow 10 minutes for cooling before serving, garnished with parsley.

INGREDIENTS IN CAPRESE QUINOA CASEROLA

• washed and drained quinoa (2 cups)

2 tbsp extra-virgin olive oil 2 minced tiny shallots

2 cups cherry tomatoes, halved • 3 garlic cloves, minced

• shredded 8 oz. part-skim mozzarella

• fresh ground black pepper • kosher salt

• 3 heirloom tomatoes, quartered

- sliced 8 oz. part-skim mozzarella

- a quarter cup of thinly sliced basil leaves

- balsamic vinegar (about 1/4 cup) DIRECTIONS

- Preheat the oven to 400 degrees and lightly grease a 9-inch pie plate.

- Cook the quinoa in 4 cups water in a large pot over medium heat for 15 minutes, until tender.

Oil should be heated in a medium skillet over medium heat. Cook for 2 minutes with the shallots and garlic. Cook, stirring, for 2 to 4 minutes after adding the cherry tomatoes.

-

Combine the quinoa, sautéed tomato mixture, mozzarella, salt, and pepper in a large mixing bowl, then transfer to a pie plate.

- Arrange the tomato and mozzarella slices in a small spiral over the filling, beginning in the center and overlapping them slightly.

30 minutes in the oven Serve with basil and balsamic vinegar drizzled on top.

INSTRUCTIONS FOR THE GREEK SALAD

SALAD PRODUCTS

1 cucumber, thinly sliced into half moons • 1 pound grape or cherry tomatoes, halved

• 3/4 cup crumbled feta cheese • 1 cup halved kalamata olives

IN ORDER TO DRESS

• red wine vinegar (2 tbsp.)

a half-juice lemon's

• Kosher salt • 1 tablespoon dried oregano

1/4 cup extra-virgin olive oil • freshly ground black pepper

DIRECTIONS

• To make the salad, toss tomatoes, cucumber, olives, and red onion together in a large mixing bowl. Fold in feta cheese with a light touch.

• Make the dressing in a small bowl: Season with salt and pepper after mixing vinegar, lemon juice, and oregano. Slowly drizzle in the olive oil, whisking constantly to ensure that it is evenly distributed.

• Toss the salad with the dressing.

INGREDIENTS FOR THE Crock-Pot Lasagna

- 1 tablespoon of extra virgin olive oil

- 1 chopped onion

- 2 crushed garlic cloves

- Kosher salt • freshly ground black pepper • 1 pound ground beef

- 1 tablespoon of Italian seasoning

- 3 1/2 cup marinara sauce (distributed)

- 16 oz. whole-milk ricotta

- 1/4 cup chopped parsley plus a little extra for garnish

- uncooked lasagna noodles from a 16-ounce box

- shredded mozzarella cheese, 4 1/2 c. DIRECTIONS

Oil should be heated in a large skillet over medium heat. Cook for 3 to 4 minutes, until onion is translucent. Cook for 1 minute, until garlic is fragrant. Season the beef with salt, pepper, and Italian seasoning before adding it to the pan. Drain grease if desired after cooking until no pink remains. Cook for an additional 2 to 3 minutes after stirring in 3 cups of marinara.

• Toss ricotta, Parmesan, and parsley in a large mixing bowl. Stir in the salt and pepper until everything is well combined.

•

Using a nonstick cooking spray or olive oil, grease the slow cooker's bowl. Make a thin layer on the bottom of the crock pot with the remaining marinara. Then layer on a layer of noodles (you may need to break some to fit), a layer of meat mixture, a layer of mozzarella, and a layer of ricotta mixture. Repeat with the remaining ingredients, ending with the mozzarella. Cook for 4 to 5 hours on low, covered.

• To serve, top with additional Parmesan and parsley.

INGREDIENTS: Eggplant Cutlets

• 2 cups dried bread crumbs • 1/2 cup all-purpose flour • 3 large eggs

1 large eggplant (approximately 1 1/4 pound) • 1 1/4 teaspoon kosher salt • 1/4 teaspoon freshly ground black pepper

- Per batch of eggplants, 1/4 cup extra-virgin olive oil

- 2 tomatoes, sliced beefsteak

- 16 fresh basil leaves • 12 oz. fresh mozzarella cheese, sliced

- 1 tsp red pepper flakes (crushed) DIRECTIONS

- To make the cutlets, preheat the oven to 350 degrees Fahrenheit. On a plate, strew flour. Whisk eggs with a fork in a shallow bowl. Mix bread crumbs, salt, and pepper together on a second plate.

- Cut the stem off the eggplant and discard it with a serrated knife. The bottom should be trimmed. Cut the eggplant into 3/8" thick rounds (or 1/4" to 1/2" thick slices).

- Dredge each slice in flour, then in beaten egg, using only one hand. Allow any excess egg to drip off before dipping into the bread crumb mixture and pressing down to help it stick. Place on a plate that hasn't been touched in a long time.

- Heat 1/4 cup of oil in a large skillet over medium heat. Cook for about 3 minutes, or until the undersides are golden brown, using tongs to add as many cutlets as will fit in a single layer (they should sizzle). Cook for another 2–3 minutes, until golden brown on the other side. Place the chicken on a plate lined with paper towels. Repeat with another 1/4 cup oil and the remaining eggplant, wiping out the skillet with paper towels.

• Preheat the oven to 400 degrees Fahrenheit (with the middle rack in the oven).

• On a rimmed sheet pan, layer the cutlets in a single layer. A slice of tomato and a slice of mozzarella should be placed on top of each one. 3 to 5 minutes in the oven until the cheese is melted Sprinkle with Parmesan and red pepper flakes before scattering the basil leaves on top.

INGREDIENTS FOR PRIMARY SKETCH PIZZA

• two sliced bell peppers

• 1/4 small red onion, thinly sliced • 1/2 broccoli head, florets removed

extra-virgin olive oil • kosher salt • 1 cup cherry tomatoes

• Black pepper, freshly ground

• Dusting surface with all-purpose flour

1 pound room-temperature pizza dough

• 1 cup ricotta • 1 cup mozzarella shredded DIRECTIONS

• Preheat oven to 400 degrees Fahrenheit (200 degrees Celsius). Season peppers, broccoli, onion, and cherry tomatoes with salt and pepper and toss them with olive oil on a large baking sheet.

• Roast for 18 to 20 minutes, or until tender and tomatoes burst. Remove the pan from the oven and raise the temperature to 500 degrees Fahrenheit.

•

Meanwhile, drizzle olive oil into an oven-safe skillet.

•

Roll out dough until it's the circumference of your skillet on a floured work surface with your hands. Brush the dough with olive oil before placing it in the skillet.

• Spread spoonfuls of ricotta on dough and top with mozzarella, leaving a 1/2" border for the crust.

Drizzle olive oil on top of the roasted vegetables. Season with salt and pepper.

• Bake for 12 minutes, or until the crust is golden brown and the cheese has melted.

INGREDIENTS: 2 pound halved Brussels sprouts • 2 tablespoons extra-virgin olive oil

• Kosher salt

• sesame oil (1 tblsp.)

• 2 garlic cloves, chopped

• cornstarch (1 tbsp.)

• 1 cup soy sauce (low sodium)

2 tsp apple cider vinegar • 1/2 cup water

• 1 tbsp. hoisin sauce

• 2 tsp. chili sauce (garlic)

• Sesame seeds (for garnish) • Crushed red pepper flakes

• Thinly sliced green onions as a garnish

• To serve, garnish with chopped roasted peanuts DIRECTIONS

Pre-heat the oven to 425 degrees Fahrenheit. Toss the Brussels with olive oil and salt and pepper on a large rimmed baking sheet.

• Cook for about 20 minutes, or until Brussels sprouts are tender and slightly crisp. Fill a large mixing bowl halfway with Brussels sprouts (but keep the baking sheet close by). The broiler should be preheated.

• In a small pan, heat sesame oil over medium heat. Cook, stirring constantly, for 1 minute, or until garlic is aromatic. Add in the cornstarch and mix well. Brown in soy sauce, water, apple cider vinegar, and hoisin sauce.

garlic chili paste, sugar Add salt, pepper, and red pepper flakes to taste. Bring the mixture to a boil, then lower to a low heat and cook for 3 minutes, or until it has thickened.

•

Toss Brussels sprouts with sauce to coat. Return the Brussels sprouts to the baking sheet and broil until glazed and sticky. Before serving, top with peanuts, sesame seeds, and green onions.

INGREDIENTS FOR STUFFED EGGPLANT PARM

- 1 1/2 cup marinara (distributed)

- 2 medium eggplants, peeled and halved

- 1 tbsp extra-virgin extra-virgin olive oil

1 medium sliced onion • 1 teaspoon dried oregano • Kosher salt

- black peppercorns, freshly ground

2 garlic cloves, minced

- 1 big egg, gently beaten

- 2 1/2 cup shredded mozzarella (distributed)

- 1/4 cup Parmesan cheese, freshly grated • 1/4 cup Italian bread crumbs

- Freshly chopped basil to serve as a garnish DIRECTIONS

- Preheat oven to 350 degrees Fahrenheit. 1 cup marinara sauce should cover the bottom of a 9x13-inch baking dish. Hollow out eggplants with a spoon, leaving a 1/2-inch thick border around the skin to make a boat; place to baking dish. • Roughly cut the eggplant flesh that was taken out. Heat oil in a large skillet over medium heat. Cook, stirring occasionally, until the onion is tender, about 5 minutes. Season with oregano, salt, and pepper before adding the diced eggplant. 3 to 4 minutes, stirring often, until golden and soft. 1 minute after adding the garlic, simmer until fragrant.

•

Toss the mixture with the tomatoes, egg, 1 cup mozzarella, and the remaining 1/2 cup marinara in a mixing bowl. Blend until smooth, then spoon into eggplant boats. • Bake for 50 minutes, or until eggplants are soft and cheese is browned.

• Before serving, garnish with basil leaves.

INGREDIENTS FOR Lasagna Roll-Ups

• 1 tbsp. extra virgin olive oil • 1/2 big onion, diced

• 3 garlic cloves, chopped • Kosher salt • black pepper, freshly ground

• red pepper flakes (1/2 tsp.)

• Baby spinach (10 oz.)

- 2 c. ricotta • 1 big egg

- 1 c. Parmesan cheese, grated

- 2 cups marinara sauce

- 2 cups mozzarella cheese DIRECTIONS: Preheat the oven to 350 degrees Fahrenheit. Cook lasagna noodles till al dente in a large saucepan of salted boiling water. • Heat the oil in a large skillet over medium heat. Season with salt, pepper, and red pepper flakes, then add the onion and garlic. Cook for approximately 5 minutes, or until onions are tender. Cook until the spinach has wilted. Remove the pan from the heat and stir in the lemon zest.

- Toss ricotta, egg, and 1/2 cup Parmesan in a large mixing bowl until well incorporated, then season with salt and pepper.

- On one side of each lasagna noodle, spread ricotta mixture. Roll up tightly with marinara and fried spinach on top.

- Spread a layer of marinara on the bottom of a big, deep baking dish. Combine the roll-ups with the other ingredients.

Fill each roll-up with additional sauce. Each wrap up should be topped with extra mozzarella and Parmesan. Cook for 20 minutes, or until bubbly and melted. Before serving, top with parsley.

INGREDIENTS: Eggplant Parmesan

3 medium eggplants, cut into coins • Kosher salt • FOR EGGPLANT

• 2 cups all-purpose flour • 6 big eggs, beaten (or water)

Panko bread crumbs (four cups)

• 2 c. grated Parmesan

• 3 c. shredded mozzarella • 1 tsp. oregano

• Frying oil (vegetable oil)

• Garnish with freshly chopped parsley

• FOR THE MARINARA MARINARA MARINARA MARINA MARINA

- extra-virgin olive oil (about 1/4 cup)

1 chopped onion

6 garlic cloves, minced

2 (28-oz.) cans crushed tomatoes • 1 teaspoon tomato paste

- 1 tsp. dried oregano • Kosher salt • 1/4 c. torn basil leaves

- Black pepper, freshly ground DIRECTIONS

- Put paper towels on a large baking sheet. Sprinkle salt on both sides of the eggplant slices and set them on a baking sheet.

a single layer of cookies on a baking pan Continue layering as required with another layer of paper towels. Allow 45 minutes for the moisture to evaporate.

- To make the marinara sauce, combine the following ingredients in a large mixing bowl Warm the olive oil in a big saucepan over medium heat. Cook for approximately 6 minutes, or until onion is soft. Cook for 1 minute with the garlic and tomato paste. Toss in the smashed tomatoes, basil, and oregano. Fill one can halfway with water, stir to release any remaining tomatoes, and add to the saucepan. 20 minutes of simmering Using salt and pepper, season to taste. (Make the sauce up to two days ahead of time.)

• Preheat the oven to 350 degrees Fahrenheit (180 degrees Celsius). In a small basin, pour flour. In a small dish, whisk the eggs with the milk. In a third shallow dish, combine the Panko, 12 cup Parmesan, and the dried oregano. Toss eggplant in flour, then in eggs, and last in the Panko mixture, working in stages. Place the cookies on a wire rack-lined baking sheet.

• Heat approximately 14 inches of oil in a big, high-sided pan over medium heat. When the oil is hot and shimmering, add the eggplant in a single layer and fry for 2 to 3 minutes each side, or until golden brown on both sides. Blot with paper towels after transferring to a wire rack. Allow time for cooling.

• Spread a thin layer of sauce over a large baking dish. Drizzle with extra sauce after layering eggplant slices on top, cutting as required. On top, shave some mozzarella and Parmesan. Stack the remaining ingredients on top of the first layer.

• Bake until the cheese is melted and the eggplant is soft, approximately 40 minutes, covered with foil on a rimmed baking sheet. Before serving, top with chopped parsley.

INGREDIENTS OF 5 CHEESE MARINARA

1 pound penne pasta • 1 tablespoon olive oil • 1 coarsely chopped onion

kosher salt • freshly ground black pepper • 2 garlic cloves, minced

1 tsp oregano (dried)

• 1 crushed tomato (28 oz.) can

• 1/4 cup mozzarella shredded; 1/4 cup fontina shredded; 1/4 cup ricotta ricotta ricotta ricotta ricotta ricotta ricotta ricotta ricotta

• 1/4 cup Parmesan cheese, grated; 1/4 cup asiago cheese, shredded

• Garnish with chopped parsley DIRECTIONS

• Cook penne according to package directions in a big saucepan of salted boiling water. Drain.

• Preheat the olive oil in a large pan over medium heat. Cook for 5 minutes, or until the onion has softened. Season with salt, pepper, and oregano after incorporating the garlic. After 1 minute, add smashed tomatoes and cook until aromatic. Cook for 10 minutes after bringing the mixture to a boil.

• Add the mozzarella, fontina, ricotta, Parmesan, and Asiago cheeses and stir to combine. Cook, stirring occasionally, until the cheese has melted and the sauce has thickened to a creamy consistency. Season to taste, and if required, add more salt and pepper. Stir in the penne until it is well covered in the sauce. Turn off the burner.

• Serve immediately, garnished with parsley.

INGREDIENTS IN SQUASH CASEROLE

• 4 tablespoons butter (distributed)

• 1 onion, diced • 2 pounds yellow squash, cut into 1/2"coins

kosher salt • freshly ground black pepper • 2 garlic cloves, minced

• 2 big eggs • 1/4 teaspoon cayenne

sour cream (1/2 cup)

- a quarter-cup of mayonnaise

- shredded Cheddar cheese (1 1/2 cup)

- 2 sleeves crumbled Ritz crackers • 1 cup freshly grated Parmesan

DIRECTIONS

- Lightly butter a medium casserole dish and preheat the oven to 350°.

2 tablespoons butter, melted in a large pan over medium heat Cook, stirring often, for approximately 8 minutes, or until the squash is soft. Season with salt, pepper, and cayenne pepper after incorporating the garlic. Allow 5 minutes for the mixture to drain in a colander over a basin. Remove the liquid from the container.

- Whisk eggs, sour cream, and mayonnaise together in a large mixing dish. Season with salt and pepper after mixing in the cheddar and Parmesan cheeses. Fold in the squash mixture gently, then transfer to the baking dish you've prepared.

- Toss the Ritz crackers with the remaining 2 tablespoons of butter. Cover casserole with the cracker mixture. Cook for approximately 20 minutes, or until golden and bubbling.

INGREDIENTS FOR FETTUCE ALFREDO

• 1/2 cup heavy cream • Kosher salt • 1 pound fettuccine

• 1/2 cup (1 stick) butter • 1/2 cup freshly grated Parmesan cheese, plus more for sprinkling

• Black pepper, freshly ground

DIRECTIONS: • 2 tbsp chopped parsley

• Cook pasta according to package directions in a big pot of salted boiling water. Drain the pasta water, reserving approximately 1 cup.

• In the meanwhile, melt the butter and cream in a large pan over medium heat. Cook until the cream is boiling and the butter has melted. Season with salt and pepper before adding the Parmesan. Allow the sauce to thicken slightly for 1 to 2 minutes. The sauce will be thin at first, but as it cools and pasta is added, it will thicken even more.

• Toss in the cooked pasta with the sauce until well coated. If the sauce is too thick, add 1 tablespoon of the conserved pasta water at a time until it reaches the desired consistency. Serve immediately with a garnish of parsley.

2 medium eggplants, approximately 6" to 8" long • kosher salt

INGREDIENTS: Eggplant Lasagna

• extra-virgin olive oil (1 tbsp.)

• minced garlic cloves (three cloves)

2 tsp. dried oregano • 1 yellow onion

• Black pepper, freshly ground

• 1 jar marinara (25 oz.) • 16 oz. whole milk ricotta

1 egg (large)

• 1 tablespoon chopped fresh parsley (plus more for garnish)

DIRECTIONS: Preheat oven to 400°F. • 4 c. shredded mozzarella

• Trim the ends off the eggplants and thinly slice them into 1/4" thick slices. Season with salt and set slices on a cooling rack. Allow for a 20-minute cooling period. Using a paper towel, pat the salted sides down. Cook for another 20 minutes after flipping and seasoning. Using a paper towel, absorb any excess moisture.

Oil should be heated in a large skillet over medium heat. After a minute, add the onions and oregano to the pan with the garlic. Cook until onions are translucent, seasoning with salt and pepper as needed. Cook, stirring constantly, until the marinara has warmed up.

• Toss ricotta, Parmesan, egg, and parsley together in a medium mixing bowl. Using salt and pepper, season to taste.

• Spread a thin layer of marinara sauce, a single layer of eggplant "noodles," a layer of ricotta mixture, and then a layer of mozzarella in a 9" x 13" casserole dish; repeat layers. Marinara sauce, mozzarella, and Parmesan cheese go on top of the final layer of eggplant.

• Bake for 35 minutes if covered with foil. Remove the foil if desired and broil for 1 to 2 minutes until golden on top. Allow to cool for 10 minutes before serving.

Flatbread with Cheesy Spinach Pesto INSTRUCTIONS

• 1/2 cup pesto • 6 ounces fresh mozzarella, shredded • 2 packaged naan flatbreads or 1 cooked thin-crust pizza crust

• crushed red pepper flakes • 1/3 cup baby spinach Preheat oven to 425 degrees Fahrenheit. Put parchment paper or a silicone baking mat on a baking sheet and set it aside.

• Evenly spread pesto on flatbreads or pizza crusts. • Bake for 10 to 13 minutes, until cheese is bubbling, then top with spinach and red pepper flakes. Remove the slices from the oven while they are still warm.

INGREDIENTS FOR Chipotle-Lime Chilaquiles

• sweet corn (two ears)

• 1/2 sweet onion, diced • 2 tbsp. extra-virgin olive oil

2 1/2 cups store-bought red salsa • 2 garlic cloves, minced

• 2 tablespoons adobo sauce chipotle peppers, minced

• 1 1/2 c chicken broth (low sodium)

• Tortilla chips, 14 oz. thick

2 limes, both juice and zest

• salt, kosher

• Black pepper, freshly ground

• crumbled 1/2 cup queso fresco

• 1 bunch fresh cilantro leaves, roughly chopped

• garnish: 1/2 avocado, thinly sliced

• Lime wedges as a finishing touch DIRECTIONS

• Preheat the oven to 375 degrees Fahrenheit (190 degrees Celsius). Corn should be seared in a large skillet over medium-high heat, turning every 2 minutes to ensure even charring. Remove the corn kernels from each cob and discard the cobs.

• In a skillet, heat the oil and cook the onion and garlic for 2–3 minutes. Cook for another 2 minutes on medium heat. Cook another 4 to 5 minutes after adding the zucchini. Toss in the corn and combine. Half of the mixture should be set aside from the skillet.

• Stir together the salsa, adobo, and broth. Bring the mixture to a boil, then add the tortilla chips one by one, folding gently to coat each one. Allow for some liquid absorption by the chips.

prior to adding anything else Continue until all of the chips have been added and mixed evenly.

• Season with salt and pepper, then gently fold in the lime zest and juice. Bake for 12 to 15 minutes, or until all liquid is absorbed. Toss remaining zucchini and corn mixture, queso fresco, sliced avocados, and cilantro on top of chilaquiles to serve. Lime wedges are optional.

Tomatoes, Garlic, and Whole Roasted Cauliflower INGREDIENTS

• 4 tbsp. extra-virgin olive oil, divided • 2 pound cherry or grape tomatoes • 4 garlic cloves, smashed and peeled

• 1 tsp kosher salt (distributed)

• 1/4 teaspoon black pepper, freshly ground; 1/4 teaspoon crushed red pepper flakes

1 medium cauliflower head (approximately 2 1/4 pound)

• paprika (1/8 tsp)

• fresh flat-leaf parsley, chopped DIRECTIONS

• Preheat the oven to 400 degrees Fahrenheit and place the middle rack in the oven. In a large baking dish, toss the tomatoes and garlic with 3 tablespoons oil, 1/4 teaspoon salt, pepper, and red pepper flakes, and season with 1/4 teaspoon salt, pepper, and red pepper flakes. Toss to evenly distribute the ingredients.

• Remove and discard the large green leaves from the cauliflower, then trim the stem to make it sit flat. Place the cauliflower in the center of the dish and push the tomatoes aside. Rub the remaining tablespoon of oil all over the cauliflower to coat it. 1/4 teaspoon salt and paprika Roast for 1 hour, or until cauliflower is tender and pierced easily with a paring knife.

• Decorate the cauliflower with parsley. Serve the cauliflower wedges alongside tomatoes and garlic.

INGREDIENTS INGREDIENTS INGREDIENTS INGREDIENTS INGREDIENTS INGRED

• 1 cauliflower head, florets

• 1 cup all-purpose flour

• garlic powder (half a teaspoon)

- fresh ground black pepper • 1/2 teaspoon kosher salt

- 1 cup cayenne pepper (such as Franks)

- melted butter (four tablespoons)

- To serve, ranch dressing

- For serving, celery sticks (optional) DIRECTIONS

- Preheat oven to 450 degrees Fahrenheit and line two large baking sheets with parchment paper. To make the batter, start by mixing all of the ingredients together Whisk flour, milk, and garlic powder together in a medium mixing bowl until smooth. Season with salt and pepper, then whisk until smooth.

- Using a fork, dredge the cauliflower in the batter until it is completely covered. Transfer to prepared baking sheets after shaking off excess batter. Cook for 20 to 25 minutes, or until the cauliflower is crispy and golden on the edges.

- Make buffalo sauce in the meantime. Combine hot sauce and melted butter in a large mixing bowl. Before serving, toss the "wings" of baked cauliflower with the sauce. If desired, add celery sticks and ranch dressing to the salad.

INGREDIENTS FOR A CLASSIC VEGAN BURGER

• 1/2 medium yellow onion, chopped • 2 garlic cloves, minced • 2 (15-oz.) cans black beans, rinsed and drained

1 egg (large)

• 1/2 cup plus 2 tablespoons mayonnaise

• bread crumbs (panko): 3/4 cup

• fresh ground black pepper • kosher salt

• 3 tbsp. ketchup • 2 tbsp. canola oil

4 buns for a hamburger

1 sliced tomato

DIRECTIONS: DIRECTIONS FOR 4 ROMAINE LETTUCE LEAVES

• Pulse the black beans, onion, and garlic together in a food processor until they are finely chopped.

• Add egg, 2 tablespoons mayonnaise, and panko to a large mixing bowl. Season with salt and pepper, then shape into four patties. Allow 15 minutes in the refrigerator to firm up.

Oil should be heated in a large skillet over medium heat. Cook for about 5 minutes per side, or until golden and heated through.

• Place a slice of cheese on top of each patty and cover with a lid to melt the cheese.

•

Combine the remaining 1/2 cup mayonnaise and the ketchup in a small bowl. Fill bottom buns with mixture, then top with burgers. Toss in the remaining bun halves, tomato, and lettuce.

INGREDIENTS FOR CREAMY ROASTED RED PEPPON PENE

• 1 tbsp. extra-virgin olive oil • 12 oz. penne • 1 onion, diced

• 2 garlic cloves, chopped

• 1 cup sliced jarred roasted red peppers • 3 cups baby spinach a half-cup of heavy cream

• 1 cup chicken broth (low sodium)

• 1 tsp red pepper flakes (crushed)

• Parmesan cheese, grated fresh DIRECTIONS

• Cook penne according to package directions until al dente in a large pot of salted boiling water. Return the pasta to the pot, reserving 1 cup of the cooking water.

• In a large skillet, heat the oil over medium heat. Cook for 5 minutes with the onion and garlic before adding the spinach and roasted red peppers. Cook for 3 minutes, or until wilted and warm.

•

Bring to a simmer after adding the heavy cream, chicken broth, and 1/4 cup pasta water.

• Season with crushed red pepper flakes after adding cooked penne to pan and stirring to coat.

Serve with a sprinkling of Parmesan cheese as a finishing touch.

• 5 c. low-sodium vegetable or chicken stock • 10 oz. jar sun-dried tomatoes packed in olive oil, chopped

- 1 garlic clove (chopped)

- 1 finely chopped large onion

- fresh ground black pepper • kosher salt

- Arborio rice (1 1/2 cup)

- 1 cup dry white wine • 1 1/2 cup pecorino cheese • 2 tablespoons unsalted butter

DIRECTIONS: • 1/4 cup fresh basil, chopped

Pre-heat the oven to 425 degrees Fahrenheit. Warm vegetable stock over low heat in a medium saucepan.

• Heat the sun-dried tomatoes, oil, garlic, onions, salt, and pepper in a small Dutch oven over medium-high heat. Cook, stirring occasionally, for 2 minutes. Stir in the rice and the wine for about 2 minutes, or until the wine has been absorbed. Reduce to low heat and ladle 3 cups warm stock in 1 cup increments into the rice, stirring constantly for 5 to 7 minutes, or until rice absorbs most of the liquid.

• Remove the lid from the Dutch oven and stir in the remaining 2 cups of stock. 15 minutes of baking

• Turn off the oven and set aside. In a large mixing bowl, cream together the cheese and butter. Add a splash of stock if the risotto becomes too thick. Serve immediately with basil garnish.

Rigatoni with Grilled Vegetables

• salt, kosher

• Rigatoni rigate (one pound)

• 2 green zucchini (quartered) "slits in the diagonal

• 1 medium eggplant, quartered "• Extra-virgin olive oil (for drizzling)
• Freshly ground black pepper rounds

• 1/4 cup fresh parsley • 3 cups marinara DIRECTIONS • Season an 8-quart stock pot with salt and bring to a boil. Cook the pasta until it is al dente, as directed on the package. • Preheat the grill to medium-high heat while the pasta is being drained. Place zucchini and eggplant slices on a rimmed sheet pan. Sprinkle with salt and pepper, then drizzle with olive oil and gently massage. Grill the vegetables in a single layer, about 2 minutes per side, until charred on both sides.

• Heat the marinara in a medium-sized pot over medium heat, stirring constantly until thoroughly heated. • Combine pasta, grilled vegetables, and parsley in a mixing bowl and toss well.

INGREDIENTS FOR ZUCCHINI MEATBALLS

• 2 garlic cloves, minced • 3 medium zucchini

• 1 c. panko breadcrumbs • 1/4 cup thinly sliced basil • 1 egg, lightly beaten

• 1/2 cup Parmesan cheese, grated

• Black pepper, freshly ground

• 2 tbsp olive oil extra-virgin

marinara sauce in a jar • Using a medium grater, grate the zucchini. A kitchen towel should be used to line a medium bowl. Zucchini, grated Toss with your hands, seasoning with salt to taste. Squeeze the zucchini by pulling up the sides of the towel and squeezing it until most of the moisture is gone. Fill a clean bowl halfway with dried zucchini. Combine the garlic, basil, egg, panko bread crumbs, and 1/4 cup Parmesan cheese in a large mixing bowl. Add salt and pepper to taste. Make small balls out of the zucchini mix. Around a dozen should suffice.

•

In a large skillet over medium heat, heat the olive oil. Cook until the meatballs are golden brown on all sides, about 8-10 minutes. On a plate with paper towels, drain the meatballs. Toss in the marinara sauce after wiping the skillet clean. Replace the zucchini meatballs in the pan and turn the heat to medium. Allow for another 3-5 minutes of simmering in the sauce, or until it is thoroughly warmed. More grated Parmesan cheese can be added at the table.

INGREDIENTS FOR STUFFED ACORN SQUASH

• 3 tbsp extra-virgin olive oil (divided) • Kosher salt

2 c. plus 2 tablespoons apple cider, divided • freshly ground black pepper • 1 cup farro

• 1/2 lb. sweet Italian sausage • 2 sprigs fresh thyme

- 1 tblsp. chopped yellow onion

2 celery stalks, chopped

- 1 teaspoon chopped fresh thyme

- 1 bunch chopped lacinato kale, stems removed

- Heat the oven to 400 degrees Fahrenheit. Squash should be halved after cutting off both ends.

-

Remove the seeds with a spoon and drizzle 2 tablespoons olive oil all over. Roast for 30-35 minutes, seasoning with salt and pepper as needed.

- In the meanwhile, prepare the farro by mixing it with 2 cups cider, 1 cup water, and thyme sprigs in a medium sauce pan. Bring to a low boil, then reduce to a low heat and cook, stirring periodically, for 25 to 30 minutes, or until liquid has evaporated and farro is soft. If the liquid has evaporated and the farro is still not soft, add a quarter cup of water at a time until the farro is tender. thyme sprigs should be removed

- Make the filling in the meanwhile by heating the remaining oil in a large pan over medium heat. Cook, tossing regularly and breaking up the sausage with a wooden spoon until brown and cooked through, about 5 minutes. • Drain most of the grease from the pan, saving approximately 1 tablespoon for frying, and place sausage on a paper-towel-lined dish. Cook for 6 minutes, until onion and celery are tender. Using salt and pepper, season to taste. Combine the garlic and thyme leaves in a bowl and stir to combine.

1 minute later, cook until aromatic.

• Stir in the greens often while it cooks. Cook for another 4 minutes, or until the kale is soft, adding the remaining 2 tablespoons cider after 4 minutes of simmering.

• Stir together the cooked farro and sausage in the pan with the veggies. Season with salt and pepper to taste. In 6 squash halves, divide the mixture evenly. Change the oven to broil and cook for 2 to 3 minutes, or until the tops are brown and the filling is heated.

INGREDIENTS FOR BUDDHA BOWL

• 1/2-inch cubes of 1 big sweet potato, peeled

• 1 medium sliced red onion

• 3 tbsp extra-virgin olive oil (distributed)

- 1 pound boneless, skinless chicken breasts • Kosher salt, freshly ground black pepper

- garlic powder (half a teaspoon)

- a half teaspoon of ginger powder

- minced garlic clove (small)

- 2 tbsp peanut butter (creamy)

1 lime, 1/4 cup juice

- 1 tablespoon soy sauce (low in salt)

- honey, 1 tbsp.

- 1 avocado, thinly sliced • 1 tbsp. toasted sesame oil

- 1 tbsp. fresh cilantro (for garnish) • 2 cups baby spinach

- 1 tblsp sesame seeds, toasted DIRECTIONS

Pre-heat the oven to 425 degrees Fahrenheit. Season sweet potatoes and onion with salt and pepper and toss with 1 tablespoon of oil on a large baking sheet. Cook for 20–25 minutes, or until vegetables are soft.

In the meanwhile, heat 1 tablespoon of oil in a large pan over medium-high heat. Garlic powder, ginger, salt, and pepper are all good options for seasoning chicken. 8 minutes each side until golden brown and no longer pink

side. Allow 10 minutes for resting before cutting.

• Combine garlic, peanut butter, lime juice, soy sauce, and honey in a small bowl and whisk to combine. Whisk in 1 tablespoon olive oil and sesame oil until smooth.

•

Top each dish with rice, sweet potato mixture, chicken, avocado, and baby spinach. Before serving, garnish with cilantro and sesame seeds and a drizzle of dressing.

INGREDIENTS OF A SALMON SALAD

• peeled and diced three big sweet potatoes (about 2 lb.)

• 2 tbsp extra-virgin olive oil • 1 small red onion, finely cut into half moons

- 1/2 cup dried cranberries • Kosher salt, freshly ground black pepper

- 1/4 cup fresh chopped parsley • 1/2 cup crumbled feta

- IN ORDER TO DRESS

1 tbsp. Dijon mustard • 2 tbsp. apple cider vinegar

- honey, 1 tbsp.

- 1 tblsp cumin powder

- 1/4 cup extra-virgin olive oil • 1/4 teaspoon ground paprika

DIRECTIONS

- Heat the oven to 400 degrees Fahrenheit. Season sweet potatoes and red onion with salt and pepper and toss in oil on a wide rimmed baking sheet.

- Arrange them in a single layer on the sheet equally. Cook for approximately 20 minutes, or until vegetables are soft. Allow 10 minutes to cool before transferring to a big mixing basin.

-

Make the dressing in the meantime: Whisk together the vinegar, mustard, honey, and spices in a small dish or a medium liquid measuring cup. Pour in the oil in a slow, steady stream, whisking consistently until it is completely emulsified. Using salt and pepper, season to taste.

• Combine sweet potatoes, cranberries, feta, and parsley in a large mixing bowl. Warm or room temperature are also acceptable serving options.

INGREDIENTS: Traditional Stuffed Peppers

• 2 tbsp extra-virgin olive oil, plus more for drizzling

• 1 finely chopped medium onion

3 garlic cloves, minced • 2 tbsp tomato paste

• 1 pound of beef (ground)

• 1 tomato diced (14.5 oz.) can

• 1/2 teaspoon oregano (dried)

6 bell peppers, tops and cores removed • Kosher salt • freshly ground black pepper

• Monterey jack cheese, shredded

• Garnish with freshly chopped parsley DIRECTIONS

• Heat the oven to 400 degrees Fahrenheit. Cook rice according to package directions in a small pot. Heat the oil in a big skillet over medium heat. 5 minutes until onion is tender Cook for a further minute, stirring in the tomato paste and garlic. Cook, breaking up the ground beef with a wooden spoon, for 6 minutes, or until it is no longer pink. Fat should be removed.

• Toss the cooked rice and diced tomatoes into the meat mixture in the pan. Oregano, salt, and pepper are used to season the dish. Allow to cook for approximately 5 minutes, or until the liquid has somewhat reduced.

• Drizzle oil over the cut side of the peppers in a 9" x 13" baking dish. Cover baking dish with foil and spoon beef mixture into each pepper, then top with Monterey jack.

• Cook for 35 minutes, or until peppers are soft. Remove the lid and continue baking for another 10 minutes, or until the cheese is bubbling.

• Before serving, top with parsley.

INGREDIENTS FOR WHITES CHICKEN CHILE

- extra-virgin olive oil (1 tbsp.)

- 1 jalapeo, seeded and chopped • 1 tiny yellow onion

- 2 garlic cloves, chopped

1 tsp oregano (dried)

- 1 tblsp cumin powder

- 2 green chilies (4.5 oz.) in can

- 3 boneless, skinless chicken breasts, halved

- Kosher salt • Freshly ground black pepper • 5 cup low-sodium chicken broth

- 2 (15 oz.) drained and washed white beans

- frozen corn, 1 1/2 c.

- 1/2 cup sour cream

- Monterey Jack cheese, shredded

- 1 tbsp. tortilla chips, crushed DIRECTIONS

- Heat the oil in a big saucepan over medium heat. Cook for 5 minutes, or until the onion and jalapeo are tender. Cook for 1 minute after adding the garlic, oregano, and cumin. Season with salt and pepper and add green chilis, chicken, and broth. Bring to a boil, then decrease heat to low and cover for 10 to 12 minutes, or until chicken is tender and fully cooked.

- Shred the chicken with two forks on a platter. Add white beans and corn to the pot again. Bring to a low boil, then reduce to a low heat and cook for 10 minutes, mashing approximately 1/4 of the beans with a wooden spoon. Remove from heat and add sour cream to the pan.

- Just before serving, ladle the chili into bowls and top with cilantro, cheese, and chips.

INGREDIENTS: 1/2 cup balsamic vinegar, 2 tablespoons honey

- 1 1/2 tablespoons mustard (whole grain)

• minced garlic cloves (three cloves)

• 4 bone-in, skin-on chicken thighs • Kosher salt • Freshly ground black pepper

• 2 c. baby red potatoes, halved (quartered if big)

DIRECTIONS: • 2 tablespoons extra-virgin olive oil, divided

Pre-heat the oven to 425 degrees Fahrenheit. Combine the balsamic vinegar, honey, mustard, and cayenne pepper in a large mixing basin.

• garlic, salt, and pepper to taste Blend everything together until it's smooth. Toss in the chicken thighs until they are completely covered in the sauce. Allow at least 20 minutes and up to 1 hour to marinate in the refrigerator.

• In the meanwhile, prepare the potatoes by combining them with the chopped rosemary in a medium mixing bowl and seasoning them with salt and pepper. Toss in 1 tablespoon of oil until everything is well coated. Remove the item from circulation.

• Heat the remaining tablespoon of oil in a large oven-safe pan over medium-high heat. Cook for 2 minutes, skin side down, then flipping and cooking for another 2 minutes. Add the potatoes and rosemary sprigs, nestling them in between the chicken.

• Bake for 20 minutes, or until the potatoes are soft and the chicken is fully cooked. (If the potatoes require more time to cook, place the chicken on a chopping board to rest while the potatoes cook.)

• Drizzle pan drippings over the chicken and potatoes.

INGREDIENTS FOR HUNTING CHICKEN CASEROLA

• 2 pound boneless skinless chicken breasts • 2 tbsp extra-virgin olive oil, divided, plus additional for baking dish

• salt, kosher

• 2 medium sweet potatoes, peeled and sliced into tiny cubes • freshly ground black pepper • 1/2 onion, chopped

• cut and quartered brussels sprouts (1 pound)

• 2 garlic cloves, chopped

• 2 tsp thyme leaves • 1 tsp paprika • 1/2 tsp cumin

- 1/2 cup low-sodium chicken broth

6 cup wild rice, cooked

- 1/2 cup cranberries (dry)

- a half-cup of almonds, sliced DIRECTIONS

- Preheat the oven to 350°F and lightly butter a 9"x13" baking dish. 1 tablespoon oil 1 tablespoon oil 1 tablespoon oil 1 tablespoon oil 1 tablespoon oil 1 tablespoon oil 1 tablespoon oil 1 tablespoon oil 1 tablespoon oil 1 tablespoon oil 1 tablespoon oil 1 tablespoon oil 1 tablespoon oil 1 tablespoon oil Add salt and pepper to the chicken. Cook the chicken in the skillet for 8 minutes each side, or until golden brown and cooked through. • Heat another tablespoon of oil over medium heat for 10 minutes before cutting into 1" pieces. Combine onions, sweet potatoes, Brussels sprouts, garlic, thyme, paprika, and cumin in a large mixing bowl. Cook for 5 minutes, seasoning with salt and pepper as needed. Cook, covered, for 5 minutes after adding 1/4 cup broth.

- Sprinkle salt and pepper over cooked rice in a large baking dish. Combine the chicken, cranberries, cooked veggies, and 1/4 cup broth in a mixing bowl. Bake for 15 to 18 minutes, or until the casserole is heated and the almonds are toasty.

INGREDIENTS FOR COOKING ACULAR SQUASH

• 2 tbsp. melted butter • 1 tbsp. packed brown sugar • 1 acorn squash, sliced in half and seeds removed

• a quarter teaspoon of cinnamon

• kosher salt in a pinch Preheat oven to 400 degrees Fahrenheit. Using a pastry brush, coat the insides of the squash halves with butter.

•

Brown sugar, cinnamon, and a touch of salt should be combined in a small bowl. Over the squash, sprinkling

• Roast squash on a large baking sheet, cut side up, for 55 to 60 minutes, or until fork tender. Salad with Parmesan Brussels Sprouts INSTRUCTIONS

• 5 tbsp extra-virgin olive oil

- Kosher salt • freshly crushed black pepper • 1/4 cup freshly chopped parsley

- halved and thinly sliced Brussels sprouts, 2 pound (about 8 cups)

- 1 cup toasted almonds, diced

pomegranate seeds (1/2 cup)

- For serving, shaved Parmesan DIRECTIONS

- Combine olive oil, lemon juice, parsley, 2 teaspoons salt, and 1 teaspoon pepper in a medium mixing basin.

- Toss in the Brussels sprouts until well-coated.

- Let settle for at least 20 minutes and up to 4 hours before serving, stirring regularly. • Before serving, fold in the almonds and pomegranate seeds and top with shaved Parmesan.

INGREDIENTS OF TURKEY Bolognese

- 3 tbsp extra-virgin olive oil (distributed)

1 small carrot (diced) • 1/2 pound ground turkey

- 1 small onion, chopped • 3 garlic cloves, minced

- fresh ground black pepper • kosher salt

- 2 bay leaves • 10 oz. pappardelle • 1 28-oz. can whole tomatoes, with juice

- a quarter cup of fresh basil, plus a little extra for garnish

- balsamic vinegar, 1 tbsp.

- Parmesan cheese, grated fresh DIRECTIONS

- Preheat 1 tablespoon olive oil in a large saucepan over medium-high heat. Cook for 6 to 7 minutes, or until the turkey is no longer pink and slightly brown, then transfer to a mixing bowl.

- Heat the saucepan over medium-high heat with the remaining 2 tablespoons olive oil. Season with salt and pepper and heat until the carrots, celery, onion, and garlic begin to soften, about 6 minutes. Use the back of a wooden spoon to gently smash tomatoes. Bring the mixture to a boil with the bay leaves, then lower to a low heat and continue to cook for 20 minutes.

• Meanwhile, prepare pappardelle until al dente, 6 to 8 minutes, in a large saucepan of salted boiling water. Return to pot after draining.

• Season with salt and pepper and stir in basil and balsamic vinegar. Remove the bay leaves and combine the sauce and pasta in a saucepan. Garnish with basil and parmesan cheese in serving dishes.

Parmesan.

INGREDIENTS TERIAKI TEMPERATURE LEAF WRAPS

• 2 1/2 teaspoons coconut sugar • 1 8-ounce package tempeh • 1/3 cup organic soy sauce*

2 teaspoons minced garlic (about 4 cloves) • 1 1/2 tablespoons sesame oil

1 tablespoon olive oil • 1/4 teaspoon powdered ginger

• 1 thinly sliced onion • 1 medium carrot, finely sliced

- 1 tsp tapioca flour

- Thinly sliced green onions as a garnish INSTRUCTIONS

- Mix soy sauce, sugar, vinegar, garlic sesame oil, and ginger together in a medium bowl or shallow plate. To combine ingredients, whisk together.

- Break up the tempeh into small pieces and toss it in the soy sauce mixture to coat it. Remove the item from circulation.

- Warm the olive oil in a medium skillet or wok over low heat. Stir in the onion Cook, stirring occasionally, for 5–7 minutes, or until the onion starts to brown. Cook for another 3-5 minutes, stirring occasionally, until carrots are softened.

- Add the tempeh mixture to the pan and stir it around. Cook for about 5 minutes, or until the tempeh begins to brown. Stir in the tapioca flour. Cook, stirring constantly for another 2-3 minutes, or until the sauce thickens.

- Fill each lettuce cup with the tempeh mixture. Serve garnished with green onions.

INGREDIENTS BLACK BEAN POWER BOWLS WITH APRICOT PESTO

- 1 medium cauliflower head, cut into florets

- paprika, 1 teaspoon

- garlic powder (1/2 teaspoon)

1 tsp onion powder

- Season to taste with salt and pepper.

- 1 cup farro (or any other grain)* (gluten-free if needed)

- Chopped kale (one bunch)

- minced garlic cloves (1–2)

- drained and rinsed 2 cups black beans

- 1 cup sauerkraut • green onions or cilantro, sliced

- To make Avocado Pesto, combine 1 avocado, 1 tablespoon of olive oil, and 1 tablespoon of lemon juice.

- 1 tablespoon basil leaves, packed

- Spinach (handful) (optional)

a half-juice lemon's

2-garlic cloves

- walnuts (about 2 tbsp.) INSTRUCTIONS

Preheat the oven to 400 degrees Fahrenheit (200 degrees Celsius). Grease a baking sheet with a light coating of cooking oil.

-

On a baking sheet, arrange cauliflower florets. Paprika, garlic powder, onion powder, salt, and pepper are sprinkled over the top. To coat everything evenly, stir everything together. Preheat oven to 350°F and bake for 20 minutes or until vegetables are tender.

- Cook farro (or other grain) as directed on the package in a medium saucepan. Fill a bowl halfway with cooked grains.

- Warm a little water in the same saucepan. Combine kale, garlic, salt, and pepper in a large mixing bowl. Cook for 5 minutes or until the kale is wilted.

- Toss kale, grains, beans, cauliflower, sauerkraut, avocado pesto, and fresh herbs into bowls.

• To make the avocado pesto, combine the avocado, basil, spinach, lemon juice, garlic, and walnuts in a blender or small food processor and blend until smooth. Pulse until smooth, adding more water if necessary.

NOTES

*Any vegetables can be roasted. Broccoli, asparagus, bell peppers, zucchini, and other vegetables are all acceptable options. * Follow the package directions for whatever grain you're using to get 2 cups of cooked grains! Rice, quinoa, buckwheat, and kamut are all excellent alternatives.

INGREDIENTS: 1 pound dry red kidney beans, soaked overnight • 2 tablespoons cooking oil INGREDIENTS: Cajun-Style Vegan Red Beans and Rice

• 1 medium chopped yellow onion

1 cored and diced green bell pepper

• 2 tablespoons fresh parsley, chopped, plus more for garnish • 2 medium celery stalks, diced • 6 garlic cloves, minced (about 1 tablespoon)

• 1 tsp. chili sauce

• 1 tsp. paprika • 1 tsp. dried thyme

• 1/2 teaspoon salt + additional salt to taste

• 1 tsp pepper, plus salt and pepper to taste

• 1/8 teaspoon cayenne pepper • 2 bay leaves

1/2 teaspoon liquid smoke • 1 1/2 cup dry brown rice (optional)

INSTRUCTIONS

• Drain and set aside kidney beans.

Add oil to a large pot and heat on medium. Add onion, bell pepper, and celery to the pan once it's hot. Cook for 8-10 minutes, or until the vegetables are tender and browned. Cook for another minute, or until the garlic is fragrant. Stir in the parsley, hot sauce, thyme, paprika, salt, and pepper until the vegetables are evenly coated. One minute of cooking

• Combine the kidney beans, bay leaves, and vegetable broth in a large mixing bowl. Bring to a boil, then reduce to a low heat and continue to cook for 1 hour and 15 minutes, covered. Remove the lid and cook for another 15 minutes, uncovered.

•

Prepare rice according to package instructions while the beans are cooking.

• When the beans are done, put about 1/4 cup in a blender or food processor and blend until smooth. Add liquid smoke to the pot (if using). Stir

• To serve, top beans with a scoop of rice and a sprig of parsley.

Ingredients FOR THE BEST VEGAN PROTEIN BURRITO

• 1 12 cup water • 34 cup white quinoa, rinsed

• 1 can drained and rinsed black beans • 14 cup chopped fresh cilantro

3 tsp lime juice 3 tsp hemp seeds

- 14-1/2 teaspoon sea salt • freshly ground black pepper, to taste

1 tablespoon lime juice • 3 cups destemmed and chopped kale

12 tablespoon olive oil • freshly ground black pepper, to taste • sea salt, to taste

1 cup quartered cherry tomatoes • For the Pico de Gallo

- 14 cup red onion, finely diced • 2 tablespoons cilantro, chopped

- To make guacamole, combine all of the ingredients in a large mixing bowl.

- 1 ripe avocado, peeled, pitted, and halved

- Additional Ingredients: sea salt (to taste)

- 4 gluten-free or sprouted-grain tortillas Instructions

• To make the Quinoa: In a small pot, combine the quinoa, water, and 14 teaspoon salt. Bring to a boil over high heat. Reduce the heat to low, cover, and cook for 10-14 minutes, until the quinoa is tender and translucent. Transfer to a big mixing bowl and fluff with a fork.

• Toss the quinoa with the black beans, cilantro, lime juice, hemp seeds, salt, and pepper. Remove the item from circulation.

• For the Kale • In a bowl, massage the chopped kale with the lime juice, olive oil, and sea salt for 2-3 minutes, or until tender. Remove the item from circulation.

• For the Pico de Gallo: In a mixing bowl, combine the cherry tomatoes, red onion, cilantro, and sea salt. Remove the item from circulation.

• To make guacamole, combine all of the ingredients in a large mixing bowl.

• Scoop the avocado flesh into a small bowl and season with salt and lime juice to taste. Smash the avocado with the back of a fork until it is the consistency you want. Remove the item from circulation.

• Burrito Assemblage

• On a clean work surface, spread one tortilla flat. The quinoa mixture, pico de gallo, guacamole, and kale go into the tortilla. Begin rolling the burrito away from you, tucking the sides in. Serve immediately by cutting in half. Repeat.

• Keep leftovers in airtight containers in the refrigerator.

Ingredients for Peanutty Quinoa Bowls for Two + How to Make Baked Tofu

3 tbsp tamari or soy sauce 1 tbsp maple syrup • 3 tbsp tamari or soy sauce

• 1 tbsp olive oil • 1 garlic clove, minced • freshly cracked black pepper

• 15 oz extra firm tofu, drained and pressed for 30 minutes before cutting into 8 slices

• In order to make the Quinoa Bowls, combine all of the ingredients in a large mixing bowl

12 cup quinoa • 1 tablespoon olive oil • 1 seeded and diced small red bell pepper

• 2 tbsp peanut butter • 1 small broccoli crown cut into florets

1 tablespoon fresh lime juice • 1 tablespoon water • 1 tablespoon tamari or soy sauce

• 12 tsp brown sugar or coconut sugar

2 tbsp chopped roasted peanuts • salt and pepper to taste Preheat oven to 400 degrees Fahrenheit for the Baked Tofu. Use oil or cooking spray to coat a baking sheet, or use parchment paper to line it.

• In a small baking dish, combine the tamari, maple syrup, olive oil, garlic, and black pepper.

• Put the tofu in the dish and marinate for 30 minutes, flipping it after 15 minutes. Almost all of the marinade should soak into the tofu.

• Bake the tofu for about 40 minutes, or until the edges are dark and the tofu is chewy, turning halfway through. Remove the item from circulation.

• In order to make the Quinoa Bowls, combine all of the ingredients in a large mixing bowl

• Follow the package recommendations for cooking quinoa in water or vegetable broth. In a medium pan over medium-high heat, warm the olive oil while the quinoa is cooking. Cook for 3 minutes, or until the red pepper has softened. In a large mixing basin, combine all of the ingredients. 2 tablespoons water + broccoli in a skillet Steam for 2 minutes, or until broccoli is tender. Combine the broccoli and pepper in a mixing basin.

•

Set aside the cooked quinoa and vegetables.

• In a small mixing bowl, stir together the peanut butter, lime juice, water, tamari, sugar, and ginger. Combine the quinoa and vegetables in a large mixing bowl and toss to combine. To taste, add salt and pepper. Divide the quinoa into two dishes, then top each with a spoonful of chopped peanuts and tofu pieces.

INGREDIENTS: Roasted Cauliflower with Balsamic Glaze
INGREDIENTS: Balsamic Glazed Cauliflower with Balsamic Glaze

1 big red onion, sliced into wedges • 1 large head cauliflower • 400 g cherry tomatoes

- 3 tablespoons extra-virgin olive oil • 225 grams trimmed green beans

- 55 g brown sugar and 240 ml balsamic vinegar

- 2 tbsp. parsley, chopped DIRECTIONS

- Preheat the oven to 200 degrees Fahrenheit (180 degrees Fahrenheit if using a fan). To make the cauliflower sit flat, cut off the leaves and stem. Combine tomatoes, onion wedges, and green beans in a large baking dish. Salt and oil the vegetables. Whisk together balsamic and brown sugar in a small saucepan over medium heat. Bring the water to a boil, then lower to a low heat. Allow 15 minutes for the liquid to decrease by half. • Brush the glaze all over the cauliflower, reserving some for basting, and roast for 1 1/2 hours, basting occasionally.

- Before serving, top with parsley.

INGREDIENTS OF VEGETABLE KEBAB

2 medium courgettes, sliced into 2.5cm thick half-moons • 285 g baby bella mushrooms, washed and halved

- 2 lemons, quartered

- 1 garlic clove, grated • 3 tbsp extra-virgin olive oil

- 1 teaspoon rosemary, oregano, or thyme, finely chopped

- 1 tsp. chili powder

- Sea salt • Black pepper, freshly ground • Soak wooden skewers in water for 30 minutes if using them. Preheat the grill to a medium-high temperature.

-

Alternate the ingredients on each skewer: courgette, mushrooms, onions, and lemon slices.

- Combine oil, garlic, herbs, and chilli flakes in a small mixing dish. Season skewers with salt and pepper after brushing all over with oil. Cook, rotating periodically, for 12 to 14 minutes, or until veggies are soft and slightly browned. Warm it up and serve.

INGREDIENTS: Cannellini Beans, Herb Sauce

5 garlic cloves, finely sliced • 450 g dry cannellini beans, soaked overnight and drained

- 1/4 tsp. to 1/2 tsp. crushed chilli flakes, to taste
- 3 rinds de parmesan (optional)

- Black pepper, freshly ground
- Parmesan cheese, grated fresh (optional)

- 15 g fresh basil, roughly chopped • 10 g fresh parsley, coarsely chopped

Extra-virgin olive oil (60 mL)

1 tsp lemon juice and 1 tsp lemon zest

- 1 tblsp. salt • 1 tblsp. crushed red pepper flakes DIRECTIONS: Preheat the oil in a big, heavy-bottomed saucepan over medium heat. Simmer for 2 to 3 minutes, until the garlic cloves are gently brown, then add the chilli flakes and cook for an additional minute.

• Bring to a boil the soaked beans, 1.5 liters of water, and parmesan rind (if using) in a saucepan. Reduce to a low heat and cook for 25 to 35 minutes, stirring regularly.

• In the meanwhile, create the herb sauce by blending basil and parsley in a food processor or blender until finely minced. Blend in the olive oil until smooth, then pour to a mixing basin and add the lemon zest and juice. • Remove the parm rind from the beans and season to taste with salt and chilli flakes, if using. Transfer the beans to a serving dish, cover with the herb sauce, and grated parmesan cheese if desired. Warm food is best.

INGREDIENTS FOR THE VEGAN PULLED JACKFRUIT BURGER • 1 tbsp. VEGETABLE OIL • 1 chopped red onion

1 smashed garlic clove

• 1/2 deseeded and coarsely chopped red chili

• 100 g BBQ sauce • 1 × 500g jar jackfruit, washed and drained

1 avocado (big)

• 1/4 red onion, coarsely chopped

• Lime juice, 12 oz

• HOW TO APPLY

• 4 brioche buns, slices of beef tomato, red onion rings, and small gem lettuce DIRECTIONS

• In a large pan, heat the oil over low-medium heat and sauté the onions for approximately 10 minutes, or until tender. Meanwhile, pick apart the jackfruit with two forks to shred it.

• To make the guacamole, mash the avocado and combine it with the chili, onion, and lime juice in a mixing bowl. Salt and pepper to taste. Remove the item from circulation.

• Cook for 2 minutes, stirring regularly, with the chilli and garlic in the pan.

• Cook for 3 minutes with the jackfruit.

• Cook for another 2 minutes with the BBQ sauce. Season to taste.

• To toast the cut sides of the brioche buns, slice them in half and toast for 2 minutes.

• To construct, lay a leaf of lettuce on the bottom brioche half, then a generous spoonful of jackfruit, an onion ring, a tomato slice, and the guacamole, before topping with the remaining brioche half.

lid.

INGREDIENTS FOR VEGAN LENTIL LASAGNE

• 2 tbsp. olive oil • 1 kilogram baby spinach leaves, thinly cut lengthwise and 1cm thick

• SAUCE MADE WITH TOMATOES AND LENTILS

• 2 tsp olive oil • 30 g fresh porcini mushrooms

2 smashed garlic cloves • 1 coarsely chopped red onion

2 sprigs rosemary leaves, peeled and neatly chopped • 1 medium carrot, finely chopped • 1 celery stalk, finely chopped

• 2 cans chopped tomatoes (400 g)

- 2 tins (400g) washed and drained lentils

- FOR THE CAULIFLOWER CASHEW CHEESE: • 2 tsp. dried oregano • 80 ml vegetable stock

- 1/2 cauliflower head (florets)

Cashews, 100 g

- 2 tbsp. nutritional yeast • 240 mL almond milk • 1 tbsp. vegan butter

- 80 mL water • Season to taste with salt and pepper

- Preheat the oven to 180°C (160°C fan) and grease a baking pan. Drizzle aubergine slices with oil and season with salt and pepper on a baking sheet. 30 minutes in the oven Remove the item and place it on the counter.

- While you're waiting for the sauce to finish, prepare it. Fill a heatproof basin with boiling water and add the porcini mushrooms. Allow for 30 minutes of rest time. Drain and finely chop the gritted water.

• In a medium-high-heat saucepan, heat the oil and add the onion, cooking for a few minutes until golden brown.

• Cook until soft, then add the garlic, carrot, celery, and rosemary. Cook for a further 5 minutes after adding the tomatoes and lentils. Season to taste with oregano, porcini mushrooms, and stock. Continue to cook on low for an additional 20 minutes.

• To prepare the cauliflower cheese, bring a large pot of water to a boil, then add the cauliflower and cashews and cook for around 5-7 minutes, or until both are soft. Drain and blend with almond milk, vegan butter, nutritional yeast, water, and salt & pepper to taste in a food processor. Until smooth, blend.

• Begin layering your lasagne in a 22 x 16cm oven-safe baking dish. Begin by laying aubergine slices over the bottom of the tray. Then put on a layer of lentil tomato sauce, a handful of spinach leaves, and a layer of cauliflower sauce. Continue until the dish is completely full. Cover with foil and top with the remaining cauliflower cheese.

• Bake for 40 minutes in a baking dish.

• Remove the cover and continue to cook for 15 minutes more, or until the top is crispy. Before slicing, let it rest for 5 minutes. Serve.

INGREDIENTS FOR THE BEST LENTIL SALAD

- 1/2 big yellow onion, chopped • 185 g cooked green lentils • 1 tablespoon extra-virgin olive oil

- Salt • Freshly ground black pepper • 1 medium carrot, coarsely sliced

- 1 tablespoon chopped fresh thyme

- smoked paprika, 1/2 teaspoon

- 10 g herbs (basil, parsley, mint, or chives) freshly chopped

- 30 g walnuts, pecans, almonds, cashews, or pistachios, chopped

VINAIGRETTE REQUIREMENTS:

- 2 tbsp. extra-virgin olive oil

- 1 teaspoon lemon zest • 1/2 shallot, smashed DIRECTIONS: Preheat the oil in a large skillet over medium heat. Season with salt and pepper, then add the onion and carrots. Cook, stirring periodically, for approximately 6 minutes, or until onions are soft and transparent. •

Cook for 1 minute, until thyme and paprika are aromatic. Remove from heat and whisk together all vinaigrette ingredients, seasoning to taste with salt and pepper.

•

Toss the carrots and onions with the lentils, herbs, almonds, and dressing in a skillet. Allow 10 minutes for the lentils to absorb the dressing after stirring everything together. Serve immediately from the serving dish.

INGREDIENTS FOR SAG ALOOP

- BASE FOR THE CURRY

- 25 g peeled and finely chopped ginger • 700 ml water

- 1/2 tsp. cumin powder • 2 onions, coarsely chopped

- Coriander powder (1/2 teaspoon)

- turmeric, 1/2 tsp

- salt (1/2 tsp.)

- Vegetable oil (50 ml)

- 800 g waxy potatoes (peeled and cut into 3 cm pieces) • 2 plum tomatoes, coarsely chopped

7 tbsp vegetable oil • 1/2 tsp turmeric

- 1/2 onion, diced • 1 green chilli, seeded and coarsely diced

- 3 garlic cloves, minced

- 1/2 teaspoon ground cumin • 2 inch piece peeled and coarsely sliced ginger

- 1 tblsp. coriander powder

- 1 teaspoon mustard seeds • 1/2 teaspoon fenugreek seeds

- 1/2 tsp chilli powder • 1 tsp garam masala

- 1/2 tablespoon tomato puree plus 3 tablespoons water

- blanched 200 g kale

- 3 teaspoons salt

DIRECTIONS: • 1 tablespoon chopped coriander

• HOW TO MAKE A CURRY BASE

In a big saucepan, heat the water. Cook, covered, for 45 minutes, until the onions are very soft. Cook for another 15 minutes with the tomatoes added.

• Remove from the heat and puree in a blender or with a hand blender until completely smooth. Now you have a basic curry basis to work with. You will have more than you need, but you may freeze it for later use.

HOW TO MAKE AN ALOO SAG

• Place your potatoes and turmeric in a large saucepan of boiling water. Cook for 20 minutes, or until the vegetables are soft but not falling apart. Allow to cool after draining.

• Heat 4 tbsp oil in a heavy-bottomed frying pan on medium heat. Cook until the potatoes are slightly browned but not falling apart, about 5 minutes. Taking it out of the pan

• Add the remaining 2 tablespoons oil, the green chili, onion, garlic, and ginger to the same pan. Cook for 2-3 minutes, or until tender.

• Next, add all of the spices and cook for approximately 30 seconds, or until they darken. To gently caramelize the onions, add tomato puree and increase the heat.

• Combine 350ml curry base, salt, potatoes, and blanched kale in a small saucepan and simmer on low for 5 minutes, or until potatoes are cooked through. Add a handful of coriander at the end. Serve.

INGREDIENTS FOR SPICY SWEET POTATO AND CHICKPEA CURRY

• 600 g peeled sweet potato cubes

• 3 tbsp. vegetable oil • 3 tsp. salt

• 1 (400g.) can chopped tomatoes • 2 tsp garam masala • 1 tsp cinnamon

• 1 tsp. mild chilli powder • 1 thumb-size piece of ginger, coarsely grated

• 1 tsp turmeric powder • 5 tsp curry powder (dry or fresh) • 5 tsp green cardamom pods

• 2 tbsp. mustard seeds (black)

- finely diced 1 medium onion

- 1 (400g.) container of chickpeas, rinsed • 3 garlic cloves, thinly diced

- 1 coconut milk tin (400ml.)

- tamarind paste (2 tblsp) (or lime juice)

150 g spinach (baby)

- 100 g roasted almond flakes • 1 small bunch coarsely chopped coriander

- Serving rice DIRECTIONS

- Preheat oven to 190 degrees Fahrenheit (170 degrees Fahrenheit fan). Toss sweet potato with half of the oil, 1 teaspoon salt, 12 teaspoon garam masala, and 12 teaspoon cinnamon in a large mixing basin. Bake for 20 minutes on a baking pan.

25 minutes, or until soft. Save it for a later time.

- Combine the chopped tomatoes, ginger, chili, turmeric, curry powder, and the remaining cinnamon and garam masala in a blender.

- Heat the remaining oil and infuse it with curry leaves, cardamom, and mustard seeds. When the mustard seeds begin to crackle, add the finely chopped onion and garlic and simmer for about 8-10 minutes, or until the onion and garlic are transparent.

• In a large mixing bowl, combine the blitzed tomato mixture, chickpeas, and 150ml water. Stir thoroughly. Simmer for 20 minutes with the lid on the pot.

• Remove the cover and add the coconut milk can and tamarind paste to the pot. Stir in the spinach, half of the coriander, and the cooked sweet potatoes, and cook for 5 minutes, or until the spinach has wilted and the sauce has somewhat reduced. To taste, add the remaining salt.

• Toss with the remaining coriander and toasted almonds and serve with rice.

INGREDIENTS FOR SUGAR POTATO FALAFFE

• 1/2 onion, sliced into 2 cm wedges • 500 g sweet potato, peeled and cubed

• 1 tblsp cumin powder

• 1/2 teaspoon cayenne pepper • 1 teaspoon ground coriander

• three peeled garlic cloves

200 ml vegetable stock • 150 g bulgur wheat

• 3 tbsp. minced parsley • 1/2 tsp. black pepper

• Vegetable oil, 2 tbsp. DIRECTIONS

• Preheat the oven to 200 degrees Fahrenheit (180 degrees Fahrenheit with the fan). 2 tbsp olive oil, cumin, coriander, and cayenne pepper, plus butternut squash, onion, and garlic Place on a baking sheet and roast for 30 to 35 minutes, until soft. Allow to cool after removing the squash from the oven.

•

In a separate saucepan, combine the bulgur wheat and vegetable stock. Bring to a boil, then reduce to a low heat and continue to cook for 6-7 minutes, or until the water has evaporated completely. Take the pan off the heat and set it aside.

•

In a food processor, pulse the butternut squash mixture for 30-40 seconds, until it is roughly combined. Remove the bulgur wheat from the processor and place it in a mixing bowl. Season with salt and pepper and mix to combine.

• Using wet hands, roll tablespoons of the mixture into balls. Press lightly to form a patty on a greaseproof baking sheet. Allow 30 minutes to chill before serving.

• Bake the falafel for 25–30 minutes, turning once, until crisp and hot all over. Serve with salad, hummus, and quinoa.

CPSIA information can be obtained
at www.ICGtesting.com
Printed in the USA
BVHW050718050122
625448BV00015B/554